MEMOIR WRITING AND ILLUSTRATING FOR CHILDREN

AND TEACHER'S GUIDE

ELIZABETH G. UHLIG

Memoir Writing and Illustrating for Children
and Teacher's Guide

Elizabeth G. Uhlig

Marble House Editions

Published By
Marble House Editions
96-09 66th Avenue, Suite 1D, Rego Park, NY 11374

Library of Congress Cataloguing-in-publication data

Uhlig, Elizabeth

Memoir Writing and Illustrating for Children / by Elizabeth Uhlig

Summary: A How-To Guide for young authors who wish to create their own illustrated family memoirs.

ISBN 0-9677047-2-3

Library of Congress Catalog Card Number
2003104425

This book is dedicated to all young writers

who have a story they want to tell.

TABLE OF CONTENTS

INTRODUCTION: A Note to Educators

CHAPTERS FOR STUDENTS:

GLOSSARY: Terms Used in this Book

TEACHER'S GUIDE: How to Enhance the Learning

WORKS REFERENCED: A Bibliography of Notable Memoirs for Children

INTRODUCTION: A NOTE TO EDUCATORS

We are fortunate to see the recent return of memoirs into our school curriculum. This literary genre, as separate from other forms of juvenile literature, nearly disappeared from our awareness for several decades.

It is a privilege to have so many books now that honor family life and allow children to take a look back into the times in which their parents and grandparents may have lived. As children become more aware of history as told from a *personal* point of view, that history becomes more real to them. With an understanding of what has happened elsewhere and at another time, children can ultimately see where they fit into the wide landscape that is our society.

When children take on the task of writing a memoir, they unleash an important skill that is often overlooked: deliberate introspection. In collecting family stories or simply writing their own, they must pass through the process of thinking about things in a different way. They start to think about how life was in times other than the present or the immediate moment.

When I wrote, illustrated and published my own family memoir, *Grandmother Mary,* I was able to utilize all the knowledge I had gleaned from listening to my mother's stories. I gained a better understanding of what had actually transpired and was able to determine whether or not there was some value in these stories that I could pass on to readers.

The results were more than gratifying. Every step of the way, from simply writing down my ideas, to creating the draft, to collecting the reference material for the illustrations, to the actual creating of the book, I was constantly reaching deeper and deeper levels of self-knowledge.

Memoir Writing and Illustrating for Children encapsulates the process of creating a memoir, making it palatable for young authors and suitable for classroom use. You will find a Teacher's Guide at the back that will enhance this process as you walk through it with your students.

May you enjoy every step of this experience!

1. What is a Memoir?

The word **memoir** comes from the French word *mémoire*, which means "memory." In English, we use the word to mean a story that tells about a piece of someone's life, a way of life, a time or a place that no longer exists.

The style of a memoir is usually narrative, as if someone were telling you a story. A memoir is meant to engage the listener or the reader, to enchant them, to help them to see and imagine what the author is telling them about.

Memoirs are born out of experiences that the author has actually lived or about which they have heard someone speak. An author can collect family stories and weave them into a memoir that will create a picture of a way of life that has disappeared. The reader is then able to share these stories handed down from one generation to another.

NOTES:

2. A Memoir is Different From a Biography

A biography is the story of a person's entire life. A memoir is just a *piece* of someone's life or a portrait of a time or place. When we read a memoir, we are, in a sense, "visiting" that time, that place, or that person in the story. We have a chance to experience a life that we have never known.

If, for example, the memoir is about our parents or grandparents, where they lived and what people did there, we will surely hear about a life that we ourselves are *not* living now. We will hear descriptions of neighborhoods and cities, traditions and everyday life that seem quite different from those we know today. This is the beauty of memoirs. We can experience times and places that we otherwise would not know.

Memoirs are valuable because they give us a "window" into the world as someone else knew it. The personal quality of the writing should make us feel like we are visiting an old friend or relative and hearing about a life that came before our own. It is almost like looking at someone else's photo album and hearing them tell us about each photo.

Although memoirs are *personal* stories, they need to have **universal value**. This means that the memoir should contain a lesson or a moral that can be applied to our lives today. It may be a lesson about kindness or courage, about cherishing family traditions or cultural customs. It may simply be a beautiful description of the rhythm of everyday life in some other place.

One of the universal values we might find is that people are very much the same, no matter where they live or when they have lived. People want their lives to have meaning. They want to love, to be loved, to feel strong, safe, creative and happy. People always value friendship, honesty and loyalty. So no matter *where* or *when* a memoir takes place, we will probably find something in it we consider to be important in life.

3. Writing Your Own Memoir

If you are going to write a memoir, what do you need to include? Like any story, your memoir needs to have a beginning, a middle and an end. Your story has to take place in a certain time period and in a particular setting. The action of the story has to happen to *someone*.

At the center of your story is the **main character**, the character around whom most of the action takes place. There should also be minor characters who contribute something to the story.

Your memoir may be accompanied by illustrations. These will help the reader visualize the setting, what the streets looked like and what people wore. If the memoir is about someone who is old now, the illustrations will show how they looked years ago, when they were young.

Beyond the building blocks of time, place, characters and illustrations, you have to have a **story line**. Something has to happen to your character and it should be something that makes the reader think and learn. It may be an event that changes the main character's point of view or helps them grow as a person. What happens to your character is what makes up your story!

One way to create a story line is to have your character face a challenge or a problem for which they need to find a solution. You will want to create a setting in which the action takes place so that this problem may be solved.

Another way to create a story line is to have a character who is simply appreciating life as it is happening. That character may take the reader on a journey to a place that they have never been before, a different neighborhood or country. Or they may take the reader to a familiar place but in a different time period. The author may let the reader in on a special relationship they have with a friend and tell them about some of the wonderful times they have spent with that friend. There are many ways to delight the reader and capture interest.

4. CONSTRUCTING YOUR STORY

Once you, the author, have decided upon a story line, you will have to consider some important questions. The first one is:

Who is telling the story? If <u>you</u> are the *narrator*, then your story will be in the *first person* and many of your sentences will contain the words "I" and "we." If the story is about your life, it should probably be written in the first person. This will convey to the reader that it is <u>your</u> memoir.

If you want it to sound as if someone <u>else</u> is telling the story, you will write it in the *third person*. You will be using more of the pronouns "he," "she" and "they." The story can still be about your life, but it will sound as if it is about someone else's life.

Some stories contain both "voices," first person and third person. The story may start in the first person and then switch to another voice. This is a bit tricky but it may be a style that works for your story.

You can decide which style you prefer as you begin to write. The narrator can be you or another character. You can even have an unidentified narrator but *someone* has to be telling the story! Think about whose voice you are going to use.

Your next question is:

To whom am I speaking? Whomever it is we are speaking to is the *target audience*. Is it young children? Is it children your own age? Your memoir should be aimed at a particular group of readers. This does not mean it cannot be enjoyed by readers of all ages. It just means that it is written with a certain age group in mind.

If you are writing for young children, you will want to keep your language simple and your sentences short. Each sentence should be short enough for the child to read in one breath.

If you are writing for children your own age, you will want speak the same way you would speak to your friends using the same level of language. When you write for older children you might want to be more descriptive than you would be if you were writing for younger children.

5. What Else Goes Into the Story?

Once you know who is telling the story and to whom it is directed, ask yourself this: *Which story am I telling?* Remember that a memoir is not a biography. It is not a full account of someone's life, but rather, just a piece of it.

You will need to carefully choose what you will include because in a memoir you cannot include *everything*. Think about the *ideas* that are most important to you, the ones you want to share with your readers. Think about the *lesson* that your story might have for your readers.

It is important that everything that happens in your story contribute to the main idea. Ask yourself as you start to write each sentence, "Does this sentence help me tell the story I want people to hear?" You do not want to include anything that will not help broadcast your message. This means that you will probably have to leave behind some parts of the real story and select only those parts that help to create the story you want to tell. You may also have to leave out some characters who are real but do not add to the story you are telling. Deciding *which* story you are telling is probably the most important step in memoir writing! When you have determined what it is you want your readers to know, to learn and to share with you, include only those characters and events that support your story.

NOTES:

6. GETTING STARTED WITH YOUR STORY

Before beginning the creative work, an author always has to ask this question: *Why am I writing this story?* The author has to consider what the message will be and if it will have some value to readers.

You may want to give your readers the benefit of a lesson the main character has learned. Or you may want to have your reader experience something wonderful as you did. Think about the "gift" you are going to give your readers and try to mold your story around that.

NOTES:

7. HOW LONG SHOULD THE STORY BE?

Your memoir does not have to be long. Some very deep and moving memoirs are short but contain a lot of important information in only a few words. Others are more descriptive with more action and characters. The length of your memoir will depend on how much you have to say.

One way to decide on the length of the memoir is to think about what time period you are going to cover. Your story may take place in one afternoon or it may tell about someone's entire childhood. When you know how much time your story covers it will be easier to create the story.

NOTES:

8. BEFORE YOU START TO WRITE

Now that you have thought about these basic questions and have come up with an idea for your memoir, there are some good steps you can take before you write your first *draft*.

It is easier to sit down and write your draft if you have first collected some interesting and detailed ideas that will grow into pieces of the story. And where will you get your ideas? Ideas can come from anywhere! They can come from your experiences of everyday life. They can come from stories you hear in your family. They can even come from dreams!

Ideas do not only come in the form of words. They can also be pictures. You may get an idea from something you see on the street, in school or in a book. Both words and pictures are important for building your story.

One thing we need to know about ideas is that if we do not "trap" them somewhere they can often fly away. So where can you put these words and pictures so that you may use them in your story?

It's a good practice to have a *writer's notebook* and a sketchbook. A small notebook with blank pages (no lines) serves as both a writer's notebook and a sketchbook. It is ideal for "trapping" your ideas in the form of words or pictures. You can carry your little book everywhere with you so that you are always ready to jot down or sketch something you see or hear that may be useful to your story. Remember, you never know when an idea will come. So you need to be ready with your writer's notebook at all times! Once you have collected a fair number of ideas, you will want to string them together to write the story you have been thinking about. But before you actually use the ideas, you should write an *outline* of the story line. Your outline is like a "skeleton" on which to hang the ideas. It tells you where the beginning, middle and end of the story will be.

When you write your outline, you need to keep in mind who your narrator will be and what message or messages you are sending out with your story.

As an example of an outline for a story we will look at the book *Miss Rumphius* by Barbara Cooney. Note that the outline includes who the narrator is and what messages the author is sending to her readers:

Narrator: The title character's grand niece who is telling this story about
her great aunt.

Messages: 1. Young people can gain wisdom from old people who have
experienced life in a meaningful way.
2. Each of us can do something to make our world more
beautiful.

Part I.: Beginning

A. Introduce the title character, Alice Rumphius, who is an old woman.
B. Give the setting, a small New England village.
   1. Alice Rumphius grew up in this town and lived with her Grandfather
   who was a painter.
   2. Alice worked in the art studio with her grandfather.
C. Flashback to Alice as a child.
   1. Alice's grandfather tells her stories of faraway places.
   2. Alice says that she will also visit faraway places and come back to live
   in this town near the sea.
   3. Grandfather says that Alice must also do something to make the world
   more beautiful. Alice agrees.
   4. Time passes and she grows up.

Part II: Middle

A. Alice is now a grownup people call "Miss Rumphius."
   1. She becomes a librarian in the town library.
   2. She decides it is time to see the world.

B. Miss Rumphius travels to several faraway places.
   1. She makes friends in her travels.
   2. She continues traveling, but hurts her back and has to return home.
   (This is the transition between the middle and the end.)

Part III: End

A. Miss Rumphius returns to the New England village and has a house by the sea.
   1. She grows a little garden and is happy but still knows she has to do
   something to make the world more beautiful.

B. The following Spring she gets sick and has to stay in bed.
   1. From her bed, she can see the flowers that she planted beginning to bloom.
      a. She wants to plant more flowers, but is still not well enough to do it.
C. Miss Rumphius recovers by springtime.
   1. She is delighted to see that, as a result of the wind, there are flowers blooming all over the town!
   2. She is inspired to send away for more flower seeds.

D. When the seeds arrive, Miss Rumphius takes long walks around the village and scatters flower seeds everywhere.
   1. She realizes this is what she is doing to make the world a more beautiful place.
   2. The flowers bloom all over the town and countryside.

E. Miss Rumphius is an old woman again as she was in the beginning of the story.
   1. She is now a friend to all the children of the village who like to visit her and hear her stories.
   2. Like her grandfather, Miss Rumphius likes to tell them that they too, must do something to make the world a more beautiful place.
   3. We come full circle as our narrator, Miss Rumphius' grand niece wonders herself how she too can make the world a more beautiful place.

You can write an outline just like this. It will help you organize your thoughts and ideas. Once you have your outline you can do this exercise:

Take all the ideas that you have stored in your small notebook and write each one on a separate 3" X 5" file card. When you have done that, lay all the cards out in front of you on a table so that you can see everything. With your outline as a guide, read each card and decide if it is a "beginning," a "middle" or an "end" idea. Sort the cards, making three separate piles.

This process takes a little while. As you read each card, you may come across some ideas that do not seem to fit into the story. Place those cards apart from the others and save them. They may be useful later or you may use them for another story.

You can also take any sketches or illustrations from your writer's notebook and put them on cards and sort them the same way: beginning, middle and end. Sketches are ideas just like your word cards and the right ones have a place somewhere in the story.

Now you will work with one pile at a time. Take all the cards that belong to the <u>beginning</u> of the story and see if you can put the ideas in some sort of sequence. You are not actually writing now. You are just stringing the ideas together to see the order in which the story will unfold. When you have pieced together all your "beginning" ideas, do the same thing with the "middle" and "end" piles.

Now go back to the beginning and read all the ideas and see if they flow in order. If they do, then your next step is to write a longer, more detailed outline. You are going to write out the ideas as sentences, beginning with the first pile of cards and adding the other two piles.

Now you should have a more detailed "skeleton" for your story. You know what happens first, next and last. You can see the order in which the events unfold and what happens to your main character. And if you have used some sketches as ideas too, then you will also know some of the pictures that will be in your story.

Take a look at your outline now and see if you can find the place where your **main message** is. Does the message emerge in the middle of the story? Is it revealed at the end? Put a circle around the text you think conveys your main message. It really doesn't matter where your message comes out, but it is important for you, the author, to know where it is. When you actually write the story, you will want to give special attention to the language that you use in that particular place, making sure that your message comes through.

9. The Story: True or Not?

Although a memoir is a true story or is at least <u>based</u> on a true story, you still may need to change some small things around to make the story line flow more smoothly. You may want to add or subtract a character, or you may want to slightly change the way an event occurred.

If a true event is too sad to include in your story, you can tell it in a gentler way. For example, you may want to change the way in which you describe how a character died, or you may not mention the death at all.

If there are too many characters to tell about, focus only on those characters who actually play a role in the story.

Whatever the changes are, it is important that your main message still come through to the reader. You may have to "fictionalize" your memoir a little, but you can still convey your message.

Sometimes there are pieces of the true story that are missing. When you ask your relatives to tell you how it was in the "old days," there may be things that they do not know or do not remember. Sometimes with old family stories, there is no one left to ask what really happened. So what will you do about the missing pieces?

One solution is to "stitch" the story together by creating a **composite character**. A composite character is a fictionalized character who is a combination of several different people who really existed. When you create a composite, you are inventing a character to help the plot of the story. Not all characters need to be real, and not all events need to be told exactly as they happened. As long as your story moves in the right direction, you can allow these fictionalized characters and events to be a part of the tale you are telling.

You may even want to include an element of fantasy in your story to give it a special flavor. Many memoirs include time travel, a character's ability to fly or experience something as if it were real even though it is only a dream. The bibliography in this book contains some good examples of memoirs that depend heavily upon fantasy. You might want to imitate this style when you write your own story.

10. FINDING A TITLE

Putting a title on your memoir is easier once the story is already written. Since you cannot always know just how your story will sound, you may want to wait until you have finished. A perfectly wonderful title will probably pop into your head once you have the story the way you want it. Sometimes authors use what is called a **working title**. This is a temporary title that you put on the work while you are writing it. Once you are done, a better title will probably emerge.

NOTES:

11. THE FIRST DRAFT

By now, you have collected your ideas and written your outline. You have put each idea on a card, sorted the cards into three main parts of the story and have taken out any ideas that do not fit the story.

Next, you rewrote the outline, piecing together the events of the story in the order that you want. You have thought about where you might have to add a composite character, change an event or leave out something that really happened because it does not help the story.

Now it is time to write the story in "story fashion" rather than in the form of an outline. You will write in full sentences that are linked to each other and make sense.

When you write the first draft, write it by hand. The hardest part may be the **opening sentence** which has to catch the reader's attention. Look at the first idea on your outline and see if you can create an opening sentence from that. This is only a draft, and you will be writing many of these so your opening sentence does not have to be perfect. Just start writing. Leave a blank line between the lines that you write so that you can make corrections and changes later on.

NOTES:

12. THE STORY BEGINS

Once you have an opening sentence, you are going to continue by concentrating on creating the beginning from your pile of file cards. Following your outline and using the ideas that you have put on your "skeleton," write one sentence after the next.

When you have written a paragraph read it back to yourself. Does it make sense? Are the sentences related to each other? Is there anything in the paragraph that should go somewhere else, perhaps later in the story? If so, remove that sentence from the story by writing it on a little card. You can set it aside for later.

Continue writing your beginning, making sure to set the time, the place and the main character. Somewhere in this beginning section you are going to have to introduce the situation that will give action to the story. You can do it as early as you like.

NOTES:

13. THE STORY CONTINUES

Now you have come to the middle part of the story. Take all the cards that belong to the "middle" category and see if you can put them in a sequence that follows your outline. You are going to string these ideas together, constructing sentences that make the story move forward. First, though, you will have to have a sentence that connects the beginning of the story to the middle. This is called a **transition**. Once you have created the transition, continue with the middle part of the story until you have used all the ideas that fit into it nicely. Remember to follow your outline. Then you will do the same thing with the last pile of cards, the end ideas. Put them in order so that the story conforms to the outline. Make sure there is a good transition between the middle section and the end section.

NOTES:

14. REVIEWING THE FIRST DRAFT

It does not matter yet if the story is not the way you want it to be. This is only a draft. It is a building block in your storywriting.

Read your story back to yourself. Now ask yourself these important questions.

Am I telling the story I wanted to tell?

Does your story seem like it is developing into the one you first had in your head? If you are not happy with the story, try to find the places where it has changed from what you thought you were going to tell. See if there is an idea or a sentence that does not fit. Change some things around, add some things if you need them. This is why you have left a blank line between each line of writing!

If your story is different from the one you started out to write, ask yourself this:

Has a better story emerged?

Maybe you like this story better than the one you thought you were writing. You may want to change your outline and write a new story. Keep on adding, subtracting and refining.

NOTES:

15. THE SECOND DRAFT

Now it is time to rewrite your draft. You are going to type it this time double spaced so that you have room again for changes and corrections. When you have done that, read it again. How does it sound? You still can add, subtract and refine!

Is your story line clear? Now here are some new questions to think about:

Is my main character consistent?

Does the character always act like the same person? Will the reader recognize this character all through the story? They need to be the right age for that part of the story, speak in a recognizable way for that character, and their personality and actions need to be consistent with the type of person you have shown them to be.

Do the other characters in the story contribute something to the main idea?

You don't want to have characters who are mentioned but do not play any role. Every character should be there for a reason.

Is my story interesting to the reader?

Will the audience want to continue reading?   One way to make your reader turn the page is to have several pages where the last sentence on the page introduces a new idea, a challenge, or some action that needs to be finished. You want to make your reader wonder what will happen next.

Deciding where the page will be turned is called **breaking the text**. The *text* is what you have written. *Breaking it* is the way you divide it up from one page to the next. To make your story interesting, break the text in a way that will make the reader want to turn the page to see what happens.

NOTES:

16. How Many Pages?

This is where you will have to make use of your math skills. You are going to divide your draft into actual "pages." Children's picture books are always made in multiples of four, so your story might be 8 pages, 16 pages or 32 pages. Based on the length of your story, you can decide if you will be making an 8-page, 16-page or 32-page book. When you break the text, think about the total number of pages you will be using.

You'll need to leave one page for the *title page* and another for the *dedication page.* You do not need to know yet what your title will be or to whom you will dedicate the story. Just leave room for these pages. Also think about how many pages or half-pages you are going to use for illustrations. (We will discuss illustrations later.)

Looking at your manuscript, draw lines under the paragraphs that will end or break each page to a new one. You may have to do this several times to make the text come out to the exact number of pages you have (8, 16 or 32 pages).

When you have done this successfully, number each block of text to its corresponding page so that you know what page it goes on. This is still just a working manuscript. When you have finished the story you may want to re-number the pages.

NOTES:

17. FINISHING THE STORY

Type your story, break your text and re-number your pages until you are happy with your story. And how will you *know* when your story is "right?" Here are questions to consider:

Has the message come through?

Think about the reason you wrote this story. You had a message to give to your readers. Is the message there? You might try reading the story to a few people and asking them what message they get from your story.

Is the voice of the narrator consistent throughout?

Has your own style of writing emerged, one that will be recognized as *your* writing? You want your entire story to sound as though the same person wrote it!

Is the story interesting and does it make sense?

Check to see that you do not have any unresolved pieces or any unanswered questions. The end of the story should answer any questions that arose during the beginning and the middle.

Do the time and place you are writing about come through to the reader?

Will your reader get a nice, clear idea of the setting? Your language, whether it is descriptive or simple will be the key to making sure the images of the time and place are understood.

When you have your final draft, check through it again and see if you still want to break the text in the same places. Adjust your page numbering for any changes you have made in the manuscript.

NOTES:

18. Illustrating the Memoir

In order to illustrate the story you will need to know what things, places and people looked like at the time that your story takes place, so that you can illustrate the scenes and characters that reveal the most about that time period: the streets, the homes and the clothes people wore. Your illustrations will convey the setting to your reader.

To make good illustrations you will need some reference material. This means pictures to refer to that will help you create your illustrations.

There is no need to illustrate *everything!* Some things, even characters, are better left to the reader's imagination. But doing the research and collecting ideas can be fun. There are many sources you can use: books, magazines, old photos, etc. Unless you are making illustrations completely from your imagination, you will probably have to do some research to make the pictures seem authentic to the time and place in which the story occurs. You can make photocopies of pictures that you think will be useful. Collect all your reference material in a folder so that you can sift through it and refer to it as you make your illustrations.

Now think about what style and **medium** would suit your memoir the best. Some of the media you might consider are pencil or colored pencil, crayons, paint, watercolor or ink. Think about the tools you like best: fine brushes, wide brushes, markers, pencils, etc. If you work with tools you like, you will have more fun.

Your illustrations do not have to be drawn or painted. You might make computer illustrations or use another medium like cut-paper collage or photocopies of old photographs. Your tools and medium should suit the mood of your story.

If you do not have an art style of your own, you can mimic one that you like. It is helpful to look at other illustrators' work to get some ideas about what style you'd like to use. All new illustrators look to professionals for inspiration!

Making Your Storyboard:

Before you make any actual illustrations, you will need to make a *storyboard*. The storyboard is a plan for the layout of pictures and text. It is based on the number of pages you story will be. You have already broken your text and divided it among the pages. Now it is time to decide which pages will have pictures. Don't forget about the illustrations for your cover, title page and dedication page. (We will discuss these pages later on.)

How many pictures do you need? Making the storyboard will help you determine this. You can make a storyboard by making miniature pages of your book using 3" X 5" file cards. Let's say you have decided upon a 16-page book. For your storyboard, you will need 8 file cards, pasted down on a stiff paper board. You will paste the cards horizontally or vertically, depending on what shape you'd like your book to be.

Once you've pasted the cards down, draw a line down the middle of each card. Now each card represents a double-page spread, like a book that is open.

Diagram #1:

Put a number in the upper left hand corner of each miniature "page." Keeping in mind the title page, the dedication page, the number of pages of text and the amount of text that you have assigned to each page, think about the illustration you are going to place on each page. Remember to use some of the pictures you collected from your writer's notebook. The amount of text you put on each page will determine how much space you will have left for the illustration on that page.

Before you do anything else, decide what size the <u>actual</u> book will be. You need to know the paper size so that you can determine how big to make the type and how big the actual illustrations will be.

Back to your storyboard: Now you are going to make tiny sketches that serve as a plan for each page. These sketches will be the guides for the larger illustrations you are going to make. The storyboard helps you plan the layout of your story in a realistic way so you can include what is important and make the story come out the way you like.

NOTES:

Diagram # 2:

When you have your storyboard ready and know what pictures will be included, you can begin to make some actual-sized sketches.

Now begin sketching. Draw your figures, your backgrounds, and put in any ideas for details. Remember, this is an *exercise* to help you plan out the illustrations. Just as you did with your draft, you are going to sketch, erase, and make many changes until you have just the right sketches.

When you have your entire set of sketches, it is time to make your actual illustrations. If you are simply not able to sketch illustrations, you will have to "commission" an artistic friend to make them for you.

Even very good artists may need to recreate their pictures many times before they come out right. As with your draft, you have to be willing to make an illustration again and again until you are happy with it.

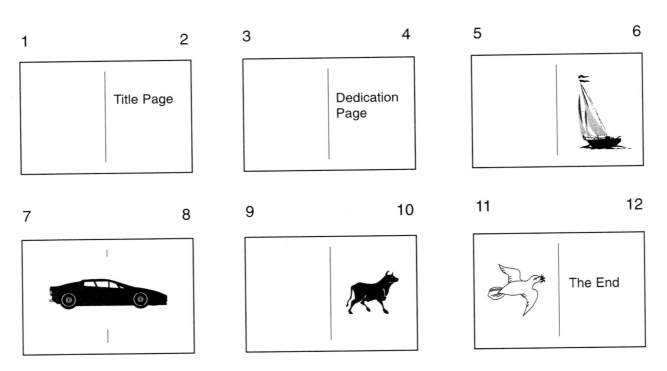

19. A Dummy of Your Book

When your storyboard and draft are ready and you have created all your illustrations, you are ready to prepare a **dummy** of your book. The dummy is a full-sized model of the book.

In order to make a dummy, you have to know:

- how much text will go on each page

- where the illustrations will go

- what the page-by-page layout of your book is, leaving blank pages for the cover, the title page and the dedication page.

Using the size paper you want your book to be, or a bound blank-page notebook, you are going to actually cut up your text and glue it to each page. You will also glue your pictures to the blank pages in the space you have allotted for them. Be sure to use rubber cement, not white glue. Rubber cement has two good qualities: it dries flat, so your text and pictures do not warp, and it allows you to remove something once it is glued down. Do not do the title page or dedication page yet. When you are finished, set the dummy aside for now.

NOTES:

20. PULLING IT ALL TOGETHER

<u>Finding a Title</u>: By the time your story is written, the title will probably have emerged. You may even have several ideas for your title. If you cannot decide which is best, ask the readers in your group which title is most appealing. This may help you make a decision.

<u>The Cover</u>: The cover of your book should have the title of the story and your name. If you are both the author and illustrator, write "Written and Illustrated by" and your name. If someone else has made the pictures, you will have their name on the cover as well. The cover illustration can be the same as one in the book or it can be something different. Choose a picture that will invite the reader to open the book.

<u>The Title Page</u>: The title page says the same thing that is written on the cover of the book: title, author and illustrator.

<u>The Dedication Page</u>: To whom will you dedicate your memoir? Authors usually choose the person or persons who have been the greatest influence on them or someone who has inspired them to write the story. The dedication page can have a small illustration to accompany your words of dedication.

<u>The Summary and Author's Bio</u>: On the back cover of your book place a short *summary* of the story that will give the reader an idea of what the memoir is about. It need only be two or three lines. Then there should also be a brief *bio* about you. You may mention where you are from, what grade you are in, what your interests are and what inspired you to write this memoir. If you have room, put a little photo of yourself on the back cover too.

NOTES:

21. YOUR FINISHED MEMOIR

Now your story has been written, illustrated and you have made a dummy with a cover. Pick up the "book" and read it aloud to yourself as if you have never heard the story before.

When you have done this, it is useful to ask yourself these questions:

How do I like this memoir?

Will others gain some benefit from my message?

Will readers learn something from my story about another time and place?

If you have put your heart into this work, you will probably have positive answers to these questions. But it is also possible that you will not be completely happy with the story. This doesn't matter. It has been a learning exercise and your next story will be even closer to what you want.

Here is a question that is more important:

Have I expressed myself artistically?

We write memoirs in order to share ideas and have our readers learn. But we also write because we, personally, have something to express in an artistic way. If you have expressed yourself through your words and pictures, you have experienced something very significant.

Here is the last important question:

What have I learned about myself by writing this memoir?

The process of collecting ideas, gathering information and putting everything in order is one in which we can learn a lot about ourselves. We can come to understand what has meaning and importance for us, what we value the most, and what we want others to know.

In completing this project you can learn about your own ability to dream up an idea and make it into something real, something that can be enjoyed by others. Perhaps you have learned that you are a more talented writer or artist than you thought previously. Or maybe you have come to appreciate what it means to write a story, to write it again and again until you are happy with it.

All creative projects help us to become more of who we are and this, in turn, gives us a greater knowledge of ourselves. As you grow, learn and experience life, your stories will change and reflect how far you have come in being able to express yourself and appreciate your own culture, history and family.

Best wishes for the journey ahead!

GLOSSARY

bio	Short for "biography." This is a short profile of the author's life and character.
breaking the text	Dividing the text of your story so that you know where a new page will begin.
composite character	A character in a book that is invented and is a combination of two more real people.
dedication page	The page after the title page on which the author has written the name of the person or persons to whom the story is dedicated.
draft	The rough, unfinished manuscript.
dummy	The model of the book, made from the pages upon which the text and illustrations have been glued.
first person	A writing style in which the author uses the pronoun "I" when narrating as if he or she were telling the story.
main character	The central character in a story around whom most of the action takes place.
main message	The author's most important idea communicated in the story.
medium	A substance or material that is used to make an illustration: paint, pencil, photographs, collage.
memoir	A story that tells about a piece of someone's life, a portrait of a time or place.
narrator	The person who is telling the story.
opening sentence	The first sentence in the story which is written to catch the reader's attention and interest.

outline	The main points and events of the story in abbreviated form in the order in which they occur.
story board	A plan for the layout of pictures and text
story line	A description in sentence form of what happens in the story.
summary	A very short version of the story that gives the reader an idea what it is about.
target audience	The readers for whom the book is written.
title page	The first page of the book that contains the same information that is on the cover: title, author, illustrator.
transition	A sentence that links one segment of the story to the next in sequence, such as the beginning to the middle or the middle to the end.
third person	A writing style in which the author uses the pronouns "he" and "she" when narrating, as if someone other than the author were telling the story.
universal value	A quality or value that can be applied or attributed to almost anyone's life. Value that is not linked to any one time or place but to life in general.
working title	A temporary title that the author has for their story until they find the one they will finally use.
writer's notebook	A small notebook/sketchbook that an author uses to collect word and picture ideas while they are getting ready to write a book or story.

TEACHER'S GUIDE

This guide follows the book chapter by chapter and will offer you suggestions for expanding your classroom work with students. You can follow along with the students and enhance their learning by supplementing the text with some of the mental and written exercises below.

References are made to children's books that you may use as examples for your students. A complete bibliography is found at the end of this book.

1. WHAT IS A MEMOIR?

This chapter serves as an introduction to the concept of memoirs and presents some ideas for motivating students to write their own. Not all memoirs have to portray a way of life that has disappeared but it helps for the students to understand that when they write a memoir, they are, in a sense, helping to preserve a memory that might otherwise be lost. In the bibliography, some good examples of books that do this are *The Piano* by William Miller and *Great Grandma Tells of Threshing Day* by Verda Cross.

Both books take place in the early part of the 20th century. With their lush illustrations and simple, touching story lines, they create portraits of times and places that no longer exist but whose memories are very vibrant in the minds of the authors.

A sample from *The Piano:*

Tia was on her way back home when she first heard the music. The melody drifted lazily across the wide, green lawn. It made Tia think of castles, mountains, and deep new snow. The music took her away from the hot, dry town.

From *Great Grandma Tells of Threshing Day:*

We children would plead each summer when we went to visit Great Grandma Swift. "Tell us about threshing day," I would add, for that was my favorite story. Rocking gently back and forth in the high-backed rocker, Great Grandma got a faraway look in her eyes. We children leaned forward in anticipation. Then she would begin.

2. A Memoir is Different From a Biography

Especially useful is to point out how a memoir can extract the thread of a story from an entire life. We are showing the children that although life is complex and full of many stories, *their* memoir is only going to focus on a particular piece of life.

Look at the book *The Saturday Kid* by Edward Sorel and Cheryl Carlesima. It gives an excellent portrait of 1930's New York through the eyes of a young boy growing up there. As big as New York is and as full and rich as this child's life is, the story focuses only on a short episode of childhood where the main character has to learn to deal with a bully. Part fantasy, part reality, the story shows us moments of life and problems that every child can relate to.

From *The Saturday Kid*:

> After school on Thursdays he would hurry off to his violin lesson. Mr. Kleinberg, his teacher, lived way downtown near Union Square. Leo would rush off to the wonderful Third Avenue elevated train that ran high above the street. It ran right next to apartment windows. Looking into people's rooms was just like watching a movie, Leo thought.

A similar example is Aliki's *Those Summers*, which offers, in both words and pictures, a beautiful portrait and cherished memory of the author's youthful days with her family.

From *Those Summers*:

> And who could forget the boardwalk - our arms linked not to separate us in the crowd. The lights, the rides, the bellowing organ music drew us as if by magic.

A different example is the simple, straightforward story, *The Two Brothers* by William Jaspersohn. Unlike *The Saturday Kid* and *Those Summers,* which take place in a brief period of time, this story covers a long stretch in the life of a German immigrant who leaves his mother and brother in Germany and comes to America. Quite by chance, the two brothers are reunited many years later. Told in highly economical language, this is a memoir that brings the reader through the youth, middle and old age of its main character with a message that hits the reader sharply and without ambiguity. It offers a superb example of what might have been a long story that the author has told in a few words.

A sample from *The Two Brothers*:

Once in a while, when the winds blew hard and the snow fell sideways, when supper was over and the dishes were cleared, one of Henry's children would say, "Papa, tell us again how you and Uncle Fred came to America." And Henry would laugh and sit back in his chair and begin: "There once were two brothers…"

<u>Universal Value</u>: Ask the children if they can suggest some values that they think are universal – those that most people would agree are worth cultivating and upholding.

Three memoirs that stimulate thought on this topic are Robert Innocenti's *Rose Blanche* which follows an episode of great courage in the life of a little girl during the Holocaust, Patricia Polacco's *The Keeping Quilt* which elucidates the value of family traditions and the cherishing of heirlooms, and Maxine Rose Schur's Jewish fable, *The Peddler's Gift,* which teaches a lesson about the strength of our own conscience and the natural human tendency to uphold ethics. Without preaching, but rather, simply by narrating, the authors of these three books convey their messages of universal value quite clearly to the reader.

A sample from *Rose Blanche*:

I walked for a long time, past the edge of town into the open fields, where I had never been. The clouds were gray. Everything was frozen. Sometimes I ran.

From *The Keeping Quilt*:

"We will make a quilt to help us always remember home," Anna's mother said. "It will be like having the family in backhome Russia dance around us at night."

From *The Peddler's Gift*:

After I had changed, the storm was still raging, so Shnook insisted I remain in the synagogue until it passed. He wrapped himself in his coat and made me sleep on his feather quilt. As we bedded down, I said, "I'm sorry I took your dreidel."

"I know you are," was all he replied.

Another universal value is that of simply <u>appreciating life</u>. The book *I Have an Aunt on Marlborough Street* by Kathryn Lasky doesn't really *tell* a story. Instead, it creates a picture of a way of life that takes place when the author, whose voice is that of a little girl, goes on one of her regular visits to her aunt. There are descriptions of the lovely, historic neighborhood in Boston where her aunt lives, the routines that the two of them enjoy together, and even a gentle observation of the patterns of nature. Although this is a somewhat plot-free memoir, there is much to learn from the sweet and endearing text as well as the softly painted pictures.

A sample from *I Have an Aunt on Marlborough Street:*

> I can touch my great grandma's initials stitched in the corner. I keep that corner near my face and I watch the moon float over the rooftops and see the chimney pots become shadowy hats against the night. Sometimes, when the moon shoots its silver light into the living room through the petticoat lampshade, the walls around me turn to lace.

Other examples of books in this category are Eve Rice's *At Grammy's House,* Marion Dane Bauer's *When I Go Camping With Grandma,* and both of Arthur Dorros' books, *Isla* and *Abuela.* These four books, all of which coincidentally share the theme of grandmothers, celebrate the main character's relationship with the grandparent and the precious time spent together. Dorros' books manage to work within the context of fantasy without missing for a moment the extraordinary relationship between the child and her grandmother.

The children will appreciate the difference in style when they read Bijou LeTord's *My Grandma Léonie.* This tiny book is an elegy or poetic tribute to a grandmother already gone and has the flavor of sadness. Both the language and the pictures are very simple, giving an excellent example of how a message can come through without a lot of words or detailed pictures.

3. WRITING YOUR OWN MEMOIR

Before getting into the technical craft of writing the memoir, have the children do some *thinking exercises* and *oral exercises* about the concepts that have been discussed so far, such as "universal value" and "visiting"

another time and place. They might reach into their own lives and give a description either verbally or in writing, as Kathryn Lasky has done, of a routine or way of life that they cherish themselves. What we are trying to cultivate here is the child's ability to acknowledge what is beautiful and meaningful in his or her own life. This sets the tone for the young author to believe that they have a story to tell, one that will be of value to someone else.

As you approach each cited work, ask the children if they can identify the main character in the story. Then ask them to identify and name some of the supporting characters. This will be good preparation for them when they construct their own stories.

This chapter discusses the idea that something needs to happen to the main character for there to be a story. The reader should be able to see a difference in the main character from the beginning of the story to the end, for whatever has happened to them will have brought about a change.

The challenge that the main character faces may be dramatic, but it does not have to be. Dramatic, serious challenges are presented in Robert Innocenti's *Rose Blanche,* a Holocaust story described earlier, Elizabeth Uhlig's *Grandmother Mary* in which the title character is given away as a child when her father is fighting in W.W. I., and Allen Say's *Grandfather's Journey*, a story of leaving home and returning once again. These three stories evoke serious emotion for the reader.

A sample from *Grandmother Mary:*

> It was so hard for Mama to raise her children alone. She especially wanted her little girl to have a better life. Mama knew that Aunt Theresa, who had no children of her own, would be able to give Mary the best of everything. So Mary was sent to live with her aunt in a fancy brownstone house on Meadow Street in New Haven.

From *Grandfather's Journey:*

> He remembered the mountains and rivers of his home.
> He surrounded himself with songbirds, but he could not forget.

The challenge does not always come as a result of such dramatic circumstances. If we look at Dayal Kaur Khalsa's delightful *How Pizza*

Came to Queens or Ellen Schwartz's humorous yet touching *Mr. Belinsky's Bagels*, we see characters, in these two cases older people, who are confronting circumstances that force them to make decisions. The way they solve their problems is somewhat painful, although the problems are not as serious as those in the books mentioned above. By comparing the stories in these two groups, children can come to understand that a character's problem or challenge can take many shapes yet be just as significant to one character as it is to another.

From *How Pizza Came to Queens,* after Mrs. Pelligrino comes from Italy:

She might just need a little time to adjust to the change," Mrs. Penny told the girls. "Let's leave her alone for a while." (But)... Even after she drank her tea, Mrs. Pelligrino still looked unhappy. Every once in a while she lifted her nose in the air and inhaled deeply. She patted her strange green package and sighed sadly. "No pizza."

From *Mr. Belinsky's Bagels,* when Mr. Belinsky is faced with the challenge of a new bakery across the street:

Mr. Belinksy made bagels. Bagels were all he made. He didn't make pies, he didn't make cakes, he didn't make doughnuts or muffins or gingerbread. He just made bagels - poppy seed, onion, and pumpernickel bagels - and he sold them in his shop, called BELINSKY's BAGELS.

Your student may choose to write a story that does not present a challenge, but rather, just shows an appreciation for life and its everyday rhythms. Books that illustrate this concept are: *Island Boy* by Barbara Cooney, *Great Grandma Tells of Threshing Day* by Verda Cross, Amy Hest's *How to Get Famous in Brooklyn* and Jonathan London's *The Sugaring-Off Party*. Point out to the students that the "memoir" aspect of these stories lies more in the author's intention to preserve in words a way of life that was significant to the people experiencing it.

How to Get Famous in Brooklyn is particularly significant because it takes place right now, and the main character is a contemporary child. She is recording everything that goes on in her neighborhood in an affectionate and highly detailed way, thereby making every feature of life in her community meaningful.

A sample from *How to Get Famous in Brooklyn:*

Bibi's Old World Bakery is where you get the best black-and-white cookies money can buy…Sunday mornings all the neighborhood kids are sent scuffling down to Bibi's - sometimes in pajama bottoms with a jacket - to get hot bagels for breakfast.

Another category of memoir mentioned in this chapter is the one in which the most important aspect is that of the special *relationship* between two or more characters. Read Deborah Hopkinson's *Fannie in the Kitchen* in which a little girl finds comfort in her relationship with the family cook and at the same time learns to cook!

From *Fannie in the Kitchen:*

Marcia liked the kitchen. Mysterious spices scented the air, and copper pans gleamed above her head like autumn moons. And Marcia decided that, after all, she liked Fannie. Fannie seemed like a magician who could make mashed potatoes fluffier than clouds and blueberry pies sweeter than a summer sky.

The value of relationships is also the main feature in *Grandaddy's Street Songs* by Monalisa DeGross, *The Two Brothers* by William Jaspersohn and *The Keeping Quilt* by Patricia Polacco. In these memoirs, although the story line is engaging, the greater value lies in what happens between the characters.

From *Granddaddy's Street Songs:*

On and on Grandaddy and I sing and call, looking at pictures of people and places from a time long ago, before I was born. And when we see the empty wagon and there is nothing more to buy or sell, we know it's time for our last call!

As your students think about the kind of memoir they will write, have them focus on what they would like to highlight: a serious, painful challenge, a not-so-serious challenge, the rhythm of everyday life, or an important relationship. Of course, a memoir may contain all of these ideas, but one will usually predominate.

4. CONSTRUCTING YOUR STORY

Review these important questions with the students before they even get started writing anything:

Who is telling the story or which voice will I use?
To whom am I speaking or who is the target audience?

With regard to the first question, a good example of a book written in the first person is Debby Atwell's *Pearl*, a memoir that covers a long time span. It is almost written like a diary. Similarly, *How to Get Famous in Brooklyn* is written diary-style. Other books already cited that are written in the first person include *Great Grandma Tells of Threshing Day*, *Grandaddy's Street Songs* and *I Have an Aunt on Marlborough Street*.

A sample from *Pearl:*

> We grew older. David got a cane, and I got a hearing aid… When we got to Alabama, David bought the first television on the block. Moving-picture shows in your own home! We met every child in the neighborhood that night. It was wonderful. The children, that is. My recollection of the television was that it was overrated. I've always preferred children to television.

For third person writing, cite *Mr. Belinsky's Bagels*, *The Saturday Kid*, *The Piano* and Cynthia Rylant's *The Old Woman Who Named Things*.

Some books contain both voices. You can cite *Grandmother Mary*, in which an unidentified first person narrator starts the story and then slips into the background. The book continues in the third person until it gets toward the end and the narrator "returns."

From *Grandmother Mary:*

> In our neighborhood everyone knows Grandmother Mary. She has lived in the house with the white picket fence for more than fifty years. On a sunny day, I may see her puttering in her garden. When I wave, her smile invites me to come and sit with her amidst the dogwoods and lilacs. It will be an afternoon of stories.
>
> [Then after the story is told] …I have enjoyed the gentle stillness of Grandmother Mary's backyard and the peaceful, sweeping sound of the

dancing trees. Birds are chirping, dusk is falling. The cat darts across the cool grass, into a bush. Inside, a lamp in one small window throws a glow on sweet, familiar things: kitchen cupboards, soft, warm chairs. The dog is snuggled up at Grandmother Mary's feet and all is well. Good night.

A child should be able to write in both first and third person voices, but for their own story, they will probably find one voice more natural and easy than the other and that is the one they should use in order to produce the best results.

Of course, when choosing a style, you will want students to take into consideration the second question - To whom am I speaking? That will determine much about both the voice and the style of language, whether it will be simple or complex. The student authors need to think about "Who is going to be reading this book?"

You can point out some good examples of simple language in *Grandfather's Journey*, *Rose Blanche*, *When Pizza Came to Queens* and Nancy White Carlson's *Grandpappy*. Notice how short, yet potent, each sentence is. For descriptive language, point to *The Piano*, *I Have an Aunt on Marlborough Street*, *Grandmother Mary*, *Fanny in the Kitchen* and *Those Summers*. Ask the children to think about the difference in these styles and what degree of descriptive or simple language would suit them the best when they write.

5. WHAT ELSE GOES INTO THE STORY?

The question, "Which story am I telling?" is so important. To choose the actual thread of the story that you will tell is difficult even for seasoned authors because there is always so much to say. Choosing which story to tell is a process of distillation and discrimination.

As the students move along with the actual writing, they will need to be reminded about including only those characters and events that are relevant to the story they have chosen to tell.

In books such as *The Two Brothers*, *When Pizza Came to Queens* and *The Keeping Quilt*, it is obvious that the authors could have gone off in many directions but instead chose to isolate a particular story line from the bigger, more inclusive story. While it is important to see the "big picture," it is more rigorous to find within it the smaller, more significant story the author wants to tell.

A sample from *The Two Brothers*, a story of German immigrants:

> He saved his wages and learned to read and write in English. He went to town meetings and celebrated the American holidays. His favorite was Independence Day. On that day there was a parade down the main street of the village, and a brass band played an evening concert on the village square.

In the process of writing a memoir, children are faced with the idea of a lesson they want to give their readers. Any of the stories cited in this book can provide you with examples of good lessons for readers.

Sometimes a story has more than one lesson. It might be an interesting exercise for the children to identify what they think the main lesson is and then, perhaps, find a second, more subtle lesson. This will help them hone in on what they want the lesson to be when they write their own stories.

6. GETTING STARTED WITH YOUR STORY

Once again, we come back to the question of "Why?" As adults, we know that sometimes we read a book or see a movie and come away wondering why the author or film maker thought they needed to create this work because we derived nothing from it. If your young authors think of the memoirs they write as "gifts" for their readers, they will be more selective about what goes into the story.

Have the children volunteer some ideas about *why* they think some of the authors of the books cited here may have written them. You can prompt the discussion by suggesting some of the reasons an author writes a memoir: to preserve family history, to enjoy the process of sharing the story itself, to capture a way of life that they think is worth telling about, or just to express their feelings about something that happened.

7. How Long Should the Story Be?

Look at the various stories and compare the time periods they cover. *The Keeping Quilt* spans many generations. *Grandmother Mary* covers almost a century. Contrast these with books like *How Pizza Came to Queens* and *The Saturday Kid* which cover a relatively short span in a child's life.

You will want to make the children aware that the story itself will dictate how much time will elapse.

8. Before You Start to Write

You can point to the main character in *How To Get Famous In Brooklyn* to see how a young author collects ideas. The little girl carries her notebook everywhere and records anything that is of interest to her.

The basis of collecting ideas is really <u>curiosity</u> and an <u>interest in life</u>. The desire to know about things, what they mean, and why events happen gives rise to an interesting outlook on life. The writer's notebook should be a repository for all observations and ideas. Not all ideas are good ideas, but the activity of collecting ideas increases creativity.

<u>The Outline</u>: Have the children make an outline of one of the stories you have read together. This will be good practice for creating an outline for their own stories.

The exercise with the file cards is designed to clarify thoughts. Oftentimes, young writers do not manage to have the end of the story agree with or reflect the beginning of the story. When each thought is isolated on its own card and then placed in sequence, it is easier for the story to flow in a sequence that makes sense.

When the children write their outlines, this is the time to look for the main message. If the child is clear about their message, the story will develop around that message. Examine some of the books listed in the bibliography and have the children articulate what they think the author's main messages are. This comes back to the question "Why am I writing this story?"

The children can write a one-line statement about a book's message. Take, for example, the story *The Old Woman Who Named Things*. This is a story about an old woman who has outlived her friends and only names things that can outlive her, such as her car, her chair and her house. Then she discovers a small brown puppy and puts off naming the dog. Finally she names the dog "Lucky." The story has a clear message that can be written as a statement: "The woman's love for the dog was greater than her fear of outliving it." A statement for the book *Isla* might be: "The little girl's love for her grandmother is so strong that the two of them can 'fly' back to Puerto Rico whenever they want in their imagination."

When children get used to stating the main message, it is easier for them to clarify their own messages.

9. THE STORY: TRUE OR NOT?

We can never really be sure how accurate a written memoir is. Since many memoirs depend upon stories that are handed down from one generation to another, we have to assume that some of the "truth" has been lost from one storyteller to the next.

An author may deliberately change elements of the story to make it flow more smoothly. In *Grandmother Mary*, much of what happens to the title character is sad, but the real story is even sadder. Some events had to be told in a "softer" way. Have the students keep in mind that when they create their stories, they are allowed to make some changes and leave certain things out if it helps to keep the story flowing.

Another question to ask is: *Are there are any missing pieces?*

Particularly with family stories there are loose ends and unresolved questions and sometimes there is no way to get the answer. Authors have to be prepared to resolve these missing pieces themselves by changing, rearranging and inventing if necessary!

Regarding fantasy, there are a few excellent examples in the bibliography. There are flying characters in both of Arthur Dorros' books, *Abuela* and *Isla*, and in Faith Ringgold's *Tar Beach*. *The Saturday Kid* has a certain

fantasy quality to it like a story that has been greatly exaggerated over time or is written to convey what the main character *wished* had happened.

Another kind of fantasy shows up in Roger Essley's **Reunion** in which the main character, a little boy, travels back in time while looking at a family photo album. This technique serves the story well because the boy is able to appreciate the time and place in which family members who came before him lived.

10. FINDING A TITLE

The working title is a useful concept because it gives the writer a guideline but does not restrict creativity. Encourage as many students as possible to come up with a working title. Make it clear that they may come up with the real title after the story is written.

11. THE FIRST DRAFT

All the preliminary thinking and writing done up to now will serve as a useful aid when students actually sit down to write the first sentence. They usually find that writing the first sentence is the most difficult step. Examine the opening sentences in the books offered here.

Some are simple statements:

"There is no such thing as a secret in Brooklyn."
    —*How to Get Famous in Brooklyn*
"In our neighborhood, everyone knows Grandmother Mary."
    —*Grandmother Mary*
"The Lupine Lady lives in a small house overlooking the sea."
    —*Miss Rumphius*

And some are more descriptive:

"I will always remember when the stars fell around me and lifted me up above the George Washington Bridge." —*Tar Beach*

"I remember those summers. We'd pile all sweaty into the car for the long drive to the seashore, to the big, shady house we shared with our relatives."
—*Those Summers*

Have the children keep in mind that the opening sentence or sentences give birth to everything that will follow. The rest of the story is going to support whatever statement was made in the beginning. The story should be thought of as "circular," bringing the reader on a journey and back home again.

12. THE STORY BEGINS

Ask the students to share their opening paragraphs. As a "test" of the quality of these writings, the students can ask one another how much information the listener has gleaned from the first paragraph. For example, "Who is the main character?" "Where does this story take place?" "When does it take place?"

They can also consider whether or not these beginning paragraphs give the reader any clue as to where the story is going to go.

13. THE STORY CONTINUES

The idea of a transition is very important. We have all read works or seen movies in which we wondered, "How did that character get there?" or have thought, "Did I miss something?" This exercise should give students the idea of a well integrated work, one in which each element counts and contributes toward the whole story.

14. REVIEWING THE FIRST DRAFT

Once the initial draft is completed, ask the children the question that is posed in this chapter: "Am I telling the story I wanted to tell?" Oftentimes, writers lose track of what they intended to write and quite a different story comes out. If the writer is following the outline they prepared, the story should stay on track.

15. The Second Draft

Review the first three questions in this chapter:

Is the story line clear?
Is the main character consistent?
Do the other characters in the story contribute something to the main idea?

The student who can answer "yes" to these questions is to be commended on achieving something that is not easy! Consistency, clarity and cohesiveness are qualities that are necessary for a story to read well.

A more subjective question is "Is the story interesting to the reader?" Many of the books in the bibliography show good examples of instances where the author makes the reader want to turn the page. Look at **When Pizza came to Queens**. The author has built up tension for the reader by describing Mrs. Pelligrino, a visitor from Italy who is unhappy but cannot explain why. She simply pats a mysterious green package and sighs, "No pizza." This is humorous in that the reader knows what pizza is but the characters in the story, who are trying hard to understand Mrs. Pelligrino's unhappiness, do not. Having no idea what pizza is, they cannot remedy the situation. Then we, as readers, take on their bewilderment and for us to help find the solution we must turn the page!

Another example to share is **Island Boy** which follows its main character, Matthias, from birth to old age. A line at the end of one page says, "One day, Matthias told himself, I will return home. And this he did." The author has piqued our curiosity to see *how* he did this.

Have the children read through some of these stories, looking for the places where the authors have built up tension and written a last line on a page that makes the reader want to keep going. Ask them to see if they, as authors, can do this in their own stories.

16. HOW MANY PAGES?

This is a good exercise for math and cognitive skills. It is the part of the creative process that requires use of the "left brain." Planning the number of pages, leaving room for pictures, and deciding where to break the text all involve organizing ability.

It is important for these young authors to know that professional authors, editors and illustrators do this exercise all the time. Illustrators, especially, need to know how many pages a book will be before they can plan the pictures.

As the students break the text and think about illustrations to accompany blocks of text, it will become apparent how many actual pages their stories will require.

This exercise adds balance to the entire process by integrating the intuitive skills necessary for storywriting with the practical skills needed for layout. This allows the student to use a variety of skills to create a "whole" project.

17. FINISHING THE WRITTEN STORY

This is a good time to break the class into small groups of three or four students and set aside a time for some shared reading and critiquing.

Make a checklist of the questions in this chapter:

You had a message to give to your readers. *Is the message there?*

Is the voice of the narrator consistent throughout?

Has your own style of writing emerged, one that will be recognized as your writing?

Is the story interesting and does it make sense?

Do the time and place you are writing about come through to the reader?

One student in each group can be the "secretary" and can record the answers that the group offers as they listen to each story. Impart to the students the idea that they are acting as an "editorial team" whose job is to offer their positive, constructive feedback to each author.

Each group can report their findings to the whole class and students can exchange ideas about what makes a story work or not work.

18. ILLUSTRATING THE MEMOIR

<u>Finding a Style</u>: By looking at a variety of picture books, students can choose a style and medium that appeals to them. Note the tremendous differences among styles, from Eliza Kleven's fabulously detailed and intricate collages found in Arthur Dorros' books, to Barbara Cooney's folk-art oil paintings, to Allen Say's precise, realistic renderings. Of course a student may already have his or her own style that would be suitable. Students can also work in author/illustrator teams.

<u>Reference Material</u>: Each student should have a folder in which to collect general reference material for the illustrations. Since the students do not know yet what actual illustrations they will be making, they should simply gather visual material that has to do with the time and place they are writing about.

Part of the benefit of this exercise is that students look into books on costume, architecture, history, etc., to find pictures that support the story. They can photocopy pictures from books that they can refer to later when they make their illustrations. They can bring in photos from home or cut pictures from magazines. Much of the reference material will not be used but it is useful for students to collect it and surround themselves with pictures from the time period. It will increase their awareness of their own stories!

<u>The Storyboard</u>: It is best if each student mounts the storyboard on a piece of oak tag. This keeps it contained. The sketches should be very simple because the real purpose of a storyboard is to plan the layout of the book. This exercise provides a different kind of activity and a nice contrast to the earlier use of more intuitive mental skills needed for collecting reference material.

<u>The Illustrations</u>: Sometimes students think that a pencil sketch gets "colored in" to make a color illustration. The sketch does NOT become the actual picture!

The sketch should be traced onto good paper so that a "real" illustration can be made. (There would be no sketch in the case of a collage.) You can have the students tape the sketch to the window and then tape the higher quality paper over it. As the light comes through the window, it allows the student to trace the sketch, leaving behind any lines that they do not want in their actual illustration. Professional illustrators have a light table which is a surface with the bulb inside. They place the sketch on the light table to trace it. In lieu of a light table, the window works just fine!

19. A DUMMY OF YOUR BOOK

By now the children have done the mental work or calculations for the dummy checklist. The next task is a physical one in which they assemble their books. Once they have done this, they are going to return to address the last details as set out in the next chapter.

20. PULLING IT ALL TOGETHER

Probably the only difficult step in this part of the process is finding the title for those authors who have not yet come up with one.

The title should have some "zip" to it. It might be either clever, emotional or intriguing (despite the fact that many of the titles in the referenced list are not!). The title should give some hint as to what lies inside the cover.

21. YOUR FINISHED MEMOIR

Apart from celebrating the creation of these books with a display and discussion, a good follow-up exercise to this project is to have students answer some of the introspective questions presented in this chapter. The questions can be written in a questionnaire format for children to complete at home or during a quiet period.

Since the nature of these questions is somewhat contemplative, students might want to have some extra time to think over their answers. You can hold an optional sharing session in the class when students have completed their questionnaires.

*   *   *   *   *   *   *

END NOTE TO TEACHERS

It is my hope that this project will have enhanced creativity and self-awareness in your classroom. In our efforts to help students develop into sensitive and thinking adults, it is paramount that we enliven their appreciation of the stories that live within them.

SUMMARY FOR CREATING YOUR ILLUSTRATED MEMOIR:
STEPS:
1. Collect ideas for your story.
2. Find a story you want to tell.
3. Create a story line in a paragraph.
4. Who is the main character?
5. What challenges does the main character face?
6. Who is telling the story?
7. In what voice am I telling the story?
8. To whom am I addressing the story
9. Which story am I telling?
10. What is my main idea?
11. Why am I writing this?
12. In what time period does the story take place?
13. Collect details in your notebook.
14. Write an outline showing beginning, middle and end of the story.
15. Find a title.
16. Write the first draft.
17. Write the second draft.
18. Finish writing the story.
19. Plan your illustrations.
20. Make your storyboard.
21. Finish your illustrations.
22. Make a dummy of your book.
23. Read it aloud and share it with others.

WORKS REFERENCED

Aliki. *Those Summers*. Illustrated by the author. New York: Harper Collins, 1996.

Atwell, Debby. *Pearl*. Illustrated by the author. Boston: Houghton Mifflin, 2001.

Bauer, Marion Dane. *When I Go Camping With Grandma*. Illustrated by Allen Garns. Bridgewater Books, 1995.

Carlson, Mary White. *Grandpappy*. Illustrated by Laurel Molk. Boston: Little, Brown and Company, 1990.

Cooney, Barbara. *Island Boy*. Illustrated by the author. New York: Viking Kestrel, 1988.

Cooney, Barbara. *Miss Rumphius*. Illustrated by the author. New York: Viking Penguin, 1982.

Cross, Verda. *Great Grandma Tells of Threshing Day*. Illustrated by Gail Owens. Morton Grove, IL: Albert Whitman, 1992.

DeGross, Monalisa. *Grandaddy's Street Songs*. Illustrated by Floyd Cooper. New York: Hyperion, 1999.

Dorros, Arthur. *Abuela*. Illustrated by Elisa Kleven. New York: Dutton Children's Books.

Dorros, Arthur. *Isla*. Illustrated by Elisa Kleven. New York: Dutton Children's Books, 1995.

Essley, Roger. *Reunion*. Illustrated by the author. New York: Green Tiger Press, 1994.

Hest, Amy. *How to Get Famous in Brooklyn*. Illustrated by Linda Dalal Sawaya. New York: Simon and Schuster, 1995.

Hopkinson, Deborah. *Fannie in the Kitchen*. Illustrated by Nancy Carpenter. New York: Atheneum, 2001.

Innocenti, Robert. *Rose Blanche*. Illustrated by the author. New York: Stewart, Tabori & Change, 1985.

Jaspersohn, William. *The Two Brothers*. Illustrated by Michael A. Donato. Middlebury, VT: The Vermont Folklife Center, 2000.

Khalsa, Dayal Kaur. *How Pizza Came to Queens*. Illustrated by the author. New York: Clarkson Potter, 1989.

Lasky, Kathryn. *I Have an Aunt on Marlborough Street*. Illustrated by Susan Guevara. New York: MacMillan, 1992.

Le Tord, Bijou. *My Grandma Léonie*. Illustrated by the author. New York: Bradbury Press, 1987.

London, Jonathan. *The Sugaring-Off Party*. Illustrated by Gilles Pelletier. New York: Dutton Children's Books, 1995.

Miller, William. *The Piano*. Illustrated by Susan Keeter. New York: Lee & Lothrop Books, 2000.

Polacco, Patricia. *The Keeping Quilt*. Illustrated by the author. New York: Simon and Schuster, 1988.

Rice, Eve. *At Grammy's House*. Illustrated by Nancy Winslow Parker. New York: Greenwillow Books, 1990.

Ringgold, Faith. ***Tar Beach.*** Illustrated by the author. New York: Crown Book, 1991.

Rylant, Cynthia. ***The Old Woman Who Named Things***. Illustrated by Kathryn Brown. New York: Harcourt Brace, 1996.

Rylant, Cynthia. ***The Relatives Came***. Illustrated by Steven Gammel. New York: Bradbury Press,1985.

Say, Allen. ***Grandfather's Journey***. Illustrated by the author. Boston: Houghton Mifflin, 1993.

Schur, Maxine Rose. ***The Peddler's Gift***. Illustrated by Bulcken Root. New York: Dial Books, 1985.

Schwartz, Ellen. ***Mr. Belinsky's Bagels***. Illustrated by Stefan Czernecki. Watertown, MA: Charlesbridge Publishing, 1997.

Sorel, Edward, and Cheryl Carlesima. ***The Saturday Kid***. Illustrated by Edward Sorel. New York: Margaret McElderry Books, 2000.

Uhlig, Elizabeth. ***Grandmother Mary***. Illustrated by the author. New York: Marble House Editions, 2000.